Top Artificial Intel

AI Operators Simplified

The ChatGTP's AI Operator
Revolution and What It Means
for You

Jaideep Parashar

Author I Keynote Speaker I Researcher

Contents

Preface

As I sit down to write this preface, I am reminded of the journey that brought us to the concept of AI Operators—a journey shaped by curiosity, innovation, and the unrelenting pursuit of progress. Artificial intelligence has always fascinated me, not just as a tool of technology but as a profound force capable of reshaping the way we live, work, and think. It is a realm where possibilities are limitless, and yet, the human touch remains central to its success.

When I first encountered the idea of an AI Operator, it struck me as a bridge between where we are and where we could be. The AI Operator isn't just another technological advancement; it's a paradigm shift that redefines how we interact with machines, automate tasks, and push the boundaries of what's possible. In its essence, the AI Operator represents not only an evolution of artificial intelligence but a reimagining of human-machine collaboration.

This book was born out of a desire to share that vision. As someone who has worked across industries, from leading a company at the forefront of AI innovation to exploring the intersections of business and technology, I've seen firsthand how powerful AI can be when aligned with human ingenuity. But I've also seen the challenges—the uncertainties, the fears, and the ethical dilemmas that come with adopting such transformative technology.

Throughout these chapters, my goal has been to demystify the AI Operator for a broad audience. Whether you're a professional curious about how this technology can revolutionize your industry, an entrepreneur looking for ways to enhance productivity, or simply someone fascinated by the future of AI, this book is for you. I've written it in a way that combines technical depth with accessibility, offering insights into the "how" and "why" of AI Operators while keeping the human experience at the forefront.

You'll find that this book is not just about technology; it's about people. It's about how AI Operators can empower individuals to achieve more, help businesses thrive, and address some of the most pressing challenges facing society. From saving time and reducing errors to unlocking new levels of creativity and innovation, the potential of AI Operators is boundless—but only if we approach their development and deployment responsibly.

The journey to understanding AI Operators is one that challenges us to think critically about the future. What roles will humans and machines play? How do we ensure that technology serves as a force for good? And how do we navigate the ethical and practical implications of a world where AI Operators become part of our everyday lives? These are not just questions for technologists or policymakers; they are questions for all of us.

Writing this book has been an incredibly personal experience. It has allowed me to reflect on my own relationship with AI and the ways it has shaped my career and aspirations. As an author, entrepreneur, and advocate for responsible AI innovation, I've always believed in the power of technology to transform lives— but only when guided by human values. My hope is that this book inspires you to think deeply about the role AI Operators can play in your life and how you can leverage their potential to create meaningful change.

As you read through the chapters, you'll notice that this book is not just a guide; it's a conversation. It's a dialogue about where we are, where we're headed, and how we can navigate this journey together. I encourage you to approach it with an open mind and a sense of curiosity, and I hope it leaves you feeling both informed and inspired.

Thank you for joining me on this exploration of AI Operators. Together, let's embrace the possibilities of this new era, ensuring that innovation and ethics go hand in hand as we shape a future that benefits everyone.

Warm regards,

Jaideep Parashar

Introduction

Artificial Intelligence has often been described as the defining technology of our era. It is reshaping industries, revolutionizing how we live, and fundamentally changing the way we interact with the digital world. Among the many advancements in AI, the concept of an AI Operator stands out as a groundbreaking innovation, bridging the gap between automation and true human-machine collaboration. This book, *Mastering the AI Operator*, is an invitation to explore this transformative technology and understand why it is poised to become an integral part of our future.

Why This Book Matters

The AI Operator is not just another step in the evolution of AI; it is a leap. Unlike traditional AI systems that are limited to specific tasks, AI Operators are designed to be adaptive, autonomous, and highly versatile. They don't just respond to commands; they anticipate needs, make decisions, and seamlessly integrate into our personal and professional lives. From automating mundane tasks to enabling complex problem-solving, AI Operators have the potential to redefine efficiency, creativity, and productivity.

However, with great potential comes great responsibility. The rise of AI Operators brings with it questions about ethics, privacy, job displacement, and the balance between automation and human oversight. This book is not only a guide to understanding AI Operators but also a thoughtful examination of their implications—both the opportunities they present and the challenges they pose.

Why You Should Read This Book

Whether you are a professional navigating the ever-changing landscape of technology, a business leader seeking to harness AI for growth, or a curious individual intrigued by the future of innovation, this book is for you. Here's what you can expect to gain:

1. **Comprehensive Understanding:** This book provides a clear and accessible explanation of what AI Operators are, how they work, and why they matter. You don't need a background in technology to grasp the concepts; the content is designed to be informative and easy to follow.
2. **Practical Applications:** Beyond theory, this book dives into real-world applications of AI Operators across industries. From healthcare and education to retail and manufacturing, you'll discover how this technology is transforming the way we work and live.
3. **Ethical and Societal Insights:** Understanding AI is not just about the technology itself but also its broader impact. This book explores the ethical considerations, challenges, and responsibilities that come with deploying AI Operators, offering a balanced perspective on their role in society.
4. **Future Outlook:** What does the future hold for AI Operators? This book explores emerging trends, technological innovations, and the potential trajectory of this groundbreaking technology, helping you stay ahead of the curve.

5. **Actionable Knowledge:** Whether you want to integrate AI Operators into your business, prepare for the workforce of the future, or simply deepen your understanding of AI, this book provides actionable insights to guide your journey.

A Personal Note

As someone who has spent years exploring the intersections of AI, business, and innovation, I've witnessed firsthand the transformative potential of this technology. Yet, I've also seen the challenges it brings—the fears of job displacement, the ethical dilemmas, and the complexities of adoption. My goal in writing this book is to demystify AI Operators and help you see them not as a threat but as an opportunity.

AI Operators are tools, but they are also much more. They are enablers that can help us unlock our potential, achieve greater efficiencies, and focus on what truly matters. They are partners that, when used responsibly, can create a better, more inclusive future.

What Lies Ahead

In the chapters that follow, we will embark on a journey to understand AI Operators from every angle. We'll start with the basics, exploring what they are and why they are needed. We'll then dive into their technological underpinnings, practical applications, and the profound impacts they have on jobs, businesses, and society. Along the way, we'll address the challenges and ethical considerations, ensuring that we approach this transformative technology with both optimism and responsibility.

This book is not just a guide; it's a conversation. It's an opportunity to think critically about the future we are building and how we can shape it together. I invite you to join me in exploring the world of AI Operators and discovering the possibilities they hold.

Let's embark on this journey together.

1. What is an AI Operator?

Introduction to AI Operators

The concept of an AI operator might sound like something out of a futuristic movie, but it is very much a reality in today's world. Imagine having an assistant who doesn't sleep, doesn't get tired, and can perform tasks with incredible accuracy and efficiency. That's what an AI operator is, but it's also much more than just a digital assistant. It's a game-changer, a tool designed to transform how we interact with technology, automate mundane tasks, and unlock new possibilities in both personal and professional life.

When I first encountered the idea of an AI operator, I was fascinated by its potential to go beyond what we traditionally think of as AI. It's not just about responding to questions or providing suggestions. An AI operator is proactive. It's a system that can execute tasks, adapt to your needs, and learn from your behavior. It's like having a super-efficient partner who's always a step ahead, ready to assist you with whatever you need.

In this chapter, I want to take you on a journey to understand what an AI operator truly is. We'll explore its basics, look at how it differs from traditional AI assistants, and examine the evolution that brought us here. By the end of this chapter, you'll not only know what an AI operator is but also why it's a revolutionary step in the world of technology.

Defining the Basics of AI Operation

To understand an AI operator, let's start with the basics. An AI operator is a semi-autonomous system that can perform tasks on behalf of its user by interacting with digital interfaces. Unlike traditional AI systems that rely on users to give specific commands or interact through pre-defined APIs, an AI operator is designed to navigate, interpret, and execute tasks on its own.

Think of it as an extension of yourself in the digital world. Need to book a flight? The AI operator can navigate a travel website, compare prices, and finalize the booking. Want to order groceries? It can fill up your virtual cart based on your previous orders and preferences, complete the payment, and schedule the delivery. The beauty of an AI operator is its ability to work across various platforms and systems, mimicking human interaction while operating at the speed and precision of a machine.

An AI operator operates on three core principles:

a. Autonomy: It doesn't just assist; it takes action. By understanding your goals and preferences, it can execute tasks independently without constant input from you.
b. Adaptability: The operator learns from your behavior, refining its processes and tailoring its actions to better suit your needs over time.
c. Integration: It seamlessly connects with different digital ecosystems, such as websites, apps, and IoT devices, creating a unified experience.

These three principles set AI operators apart from traditional AI systems, making them indispensable tools in today's fast-paced digital landscape.

Evolution of AI: From Assistants to Operators

To appreciate how revolutionary AI operators are, it's essential to understand their evolution. Artificial Intelligence has come a long way, and each stage of its development has brought us closer to the concept of an AI operator.

The Early Days: In the beginning, AI systems were simple rule-based programs. They followed pre-defined algorithms and could only perform tasks they were explicitly programmed to do. These systems were limited in scope and required extensive human intervention.

The Age of Digital Assistants: The introduction of digital assistants like Siri, Alexa, and Google Assistant marked a significant milestone. These systems could understand natural language, answer questions, and perform basic tasks like setting reminders or playing music. However, they were still reactive rather than proactive. They waited for commands and operated within predefined boundaries.

The Rise of Smart AI Systems: With advancements in machine learning and neural networks, AI systems became smarter. They could analyze data, identify patterns, and provide more personalized experiences. This was the era when AI started moving beyond simple assistants to become problem-solvers. ChatGPT, for example, could generate human-like responses and assist in creative and professional tasks.

The Emergence of AI Operators: The AI operator represents the next phase in this evolution. It goes beyond providing assistance to taking initiative. It's not just a helper; it's an enabler. By combining the conversational abilities of AI with the operational functionality of digital agents, AI operators can execute complex workflows, navigate digital interfaces, and even make decisions in real-time.

This evolution is not just about technological advancements; it's about shifting the way we interact with technology. AI operators bring us closer to a world where machines can truly collaborate with humans, enhancing our capabilities rather than simply replacing them.

Key Components of an AI Operator

To understand what makes an AI operator so effective, let's break down its key components:

    a.   Natural Language Understanding (NLU):

At its core, an AI operator must understand what the user wants. NLU enables it to process and interpret natural language, ensuring that it can follow instructions, ask clarifying questions, and provide meaningful responses.

    b.   Task Automation Engine:

This is the brain behind the operator's ability to perform tasks. It integrates machine learning algorithms with rule-based systems to execute actions efficiently. From filling out forms to navigating websites, the task automation engine ensures smooth execution.

    c.   Visual Input and Processing:

Unlike traditional AI systems that rely on APIs, AI operators can interact with graphical user interfaces (GUIs). They use advanced vision capabilities to interpret screen content, click buttons, type inputs, and navigate digital environments just like a human user would.

    d.   User Behavior Modeling:

AI operators learn from user interactions. By analyzing patterns, preferences, and habits, they can predict user needs and proactively offer solutions or suggestions. This personalization is what makes them truly indispensable.

e. Secure Data Handling:

With great power comes great responsibility. AI operators are designed with robust security measures to handle sensitive information safely. End-to-end encryption, user-specific access controls, and activity monitoring are essential components.

f. Integration Layer:

The operator's ability to connect with multiple platforms and ecosystems is crucial. Whether it's navigating a website, interacting with IoT devices, or integrating with enterprise software, the integration layer ensures seamless functionality.

These components work together to create a system that is not only intelligent but also highly practical. They enable the AI operator to go beyond mere assistance and become a true partner in achieving goals and solving problems.

Final Thoughts

The AI operator is not just a technological advancement; it's a paradigm shift. It represents a future where machines are not just tools but collaborators. As we delve deeper into this book, you'll discover how AI operators are poised to transform industries, enhance personal productivity, and redefine the boundaries of what's possible.

In this chapter, we've laid the foundation by understanding what an AI operator is, how it evolved, and what makes it unique. In the next chapters, we'll explore the needs driving this innovation, the challenges it addresses, and the profound impact it can have on our lives. For now, let's embrace the fact that we are standing at the brink of a new era—one where AI operators are set to become our most trusted allies in navigating the complexities of the modern world.

2. The Need for an AI Operator

Why Current AI Tools Fall Short

Artificial Intelligence (AI) has become a part of our everyday lives, from chatbots answering customer service queries to smart assistants like Alexa and Siri helping us with daily tasks. While these tools are impressive, they are far from perfect. For all their capabilities, traditional AI systems often fall short of meeting the complex demands of modern life and business. This gap is what drives the need for an AI operator—a tool that goes beyond limitations to become a proactive, reliable partner.

Let's start with the most common AI tools we use today. They are great at providing answers, setting reminders, and automating simple processes. But the reality is that these systems are reactive. They wait for us to give them commands, and even then, their responses are often confined to a predefined scope. For instance, a chatbot might answer a basic question but fail when faced with a slightly unconventional query. Similarly, a smart assistant might remind you of a meeting but won't help you prepare the materials for it or book the transportation required to get there.

This is the crux of the issue: Current AI tools lack the autonomy, adaptability, and depth needed to truly transform the way we live and work. They require constant human input to function effectively, which limits their potential and places unnecessary strain on users. These shortcomings underline the necessity for a more advanced solution, one that can bridge the gap between simple automation and true operational intelligence.

Challenges and Limitations of Traditional AI Systems

Traditional AI systems face several challenges that prevent them from fulfilling their potential. Understanding these limitations helps us see why an AI operator is not just a luxury but a necessity in the modern world.

    a.   Limited Autonomy

Most AI systems are designed to operate within fixed parameters. They excel at performing repetitive tasks but falter when faced with new or complex situations. For instance, an AI-powered virtual assistant can set up an appointment, but it cannot independently resolve scheduling conflicts or negotiate times with multiple parties. This lack of autonomy means that humans must constantly supervise and guide the system, defeating the purpose of automation.

b. Inflexibility

AI systems often struggle to adapt to changing environments or user preferences. A chatbot trained to handle customer inquiries for a retail store might fail when the store expands into new product categories. Retraining the system can be time-consuming and costly, making traditional AI tools less scalable.

c. Narrow Scope

Traditional AI systems are typically designed for specific tasks. They cannot easily transition from one domain to another. For example, an AI system built to manage inventory cannot be repurposed to handle customer support without significant reengineering. This narrow scope limits their usability and effectiveness.

d. Dependence on APIs

Many AI systems rely on APIs to interact with other platforms. While APIs are useful, they create dependencies and limit the AI's ability to operate in environments where APIs are unavailable. For example, if a platform changes its API structure or restricts access, the AI system becomes obsolete.

e.   Lack of Proactivity

Traditional AI systems are reactive by nature. They wait for users to initiate interactions and provide inputs. This reactive approach places the burden of decision-making on the user and reduces the system's overall efficiency.

The Role of AI Operators in Addressing Existing Gaps

This is where AI operators come into play. Unlike traditional AI systems, AI operators are designed to address these challenges by combining autonomy, adaptability, and intelligence. They are not just tools; they are collaborators capable of performing tasks, making decisions, and learning from their environment. Here's how AI operators fill the gaps left by traditional AI systems:

a.   Enhanced Autonomy

An AI operator doesn't wait for instructions; it takes initiative. For example, if you need to book a flight, an AI operator won't just find flights; it will compare prices, consider your preferences, and even finalize the booking on your behalf. This level of autonomy reduces the need for constant user input and frees up time for more important tasks.

b. Adaptability to Dynamic Environments

AI operators are designed to adapt to changing environments and user needs. They learn from interactions, analyze patterns, and adjust their behavior accordingly. For instance, an AI operator managing inventory in a warehouse can adapt to seasonal demand fluctuations without requiring manual reprogramming.

c. Comprehensive Task Handling

Unlike traditional systems with narrow scopes, AI operators can handle a wide range of tasks. From automating workflows to managing complex projects, they offer a level of versatility that traditional AI tools cannot match. This makes them invaluable in industries like healthcare, finance, and logistics.

d. Freedom from API Dependence

AI operators can interact directly with graphical user interfaces (GUIs) using visual input and processing. This capability allows them to navigate websites, fill out forms, and complete transactions without relying on APIs. This makes them more robust and versatile in environments where API access is limited or unavailable.

    e.   Proactive Functionality

One of the most significant advantages of an AI operator is its proactivity. Instead of waiting for user commands, it anticipates needs and acts accordingly. For example, it might remind you of an upcoming deadline and automatically gather the required documents or information to help you meet it.

A Vision for the Future of AI Integration

The advent of AI operators represents a new chapter in the evolution of artificial intelligence. It's not just about making systems smarter; it's about making them more human-like in their ability to collaborate, adapt, and deliver results. Here's a vision of how AI operators can transform the future:

    a.   Empowering Individuals

Imagine having an AI operator that handles all your mundane tasks, from scheduling appointments to managing your finances. This would free up time for creativity, learning, and personal growth. It's not about replacing humans but empowering them to focus on what truly matters.

b. Revolutionizing Businesses

For businesses, AI operators can streamline operations, reduce costs, and enhance customer experiences. From automating supply chain management to personalizing marketing campaigns, the possibilities are endless. Companies that adopt AI operators will gain a competitive edge in their respective industries.

c. Creating Inclusive AI Ecosystems

AI operators have the potential to democratize access to advanced AI capabilities. By making these tools affordable and user-friendly, we can ensure that small businesses, startups, and individuals benefit just as much as large corporations.

d. Shaping Ethical AI Development

As we integrate AI operators into our lives, it's crucial to address ethical considerations. This includes ensuring data privacy, preventing bias, and creating systems that prioritize human well-being. The future of AI should be guided by principles that promote fairness, transparency, and inclusivity.

Final Thoughts

The need for an AI operator is not just a response to the limitations of traditional AI systems; it's a recognition of the evolving demands of our digital age. As technology becomes more complex, our tools must become more intuitive, adaptive, and capable. AI operators represent the next step in this journey, bridging the gap between human potential and machine efficiency.

In this chapter, we explored why traditional AI tools fall short, the challenges they face, and how AI operators address these gaps. We also looked ahead to a future where AI operators empower individuals, transform businesses, and shape a more inclusive and ethical AI ecosystem. As we move forward, the question is no longer whether we need AI operators, but how we can maximize their potential to create a better, more efficient world.

3. Objectives of the AI Operator

Resolving Challenges in Current AI Systems

Artificial Intelligence (AI) has undeniably transformed how we live and work. From virtual assistants to recommendation engines, AI has seeped into every corner of our daily routines. However, as advanced as AI systems have become, they are far from perfect. The limitations of current AI systems are glaring when it comes to autonomy, adaptability, and scalability. This is where the AI Operator steps in, addressing the challenges that have held traditional AI back.

One of the most pressing issues with current AI systems is their inability to operate beyond predefined parameters. Traditional AI can answer questions, execute specific tasks, and even generate creative content. Yet, it often falters when faced with scenarios outside its programming. For instance, a chatbot might excel at answering frequently asked questions but struggle to handle unique customer complaints. Similarly, virtual assistants like Siri and Alexa are great for setting reminders or playing music but fail to execute more complex, multi-step tasks.

The AI Operator resolves these challenges by introducing a higher level of autonomy. Unlike traditional AI systems, the Operator doesn't require constant user input. Instead, it anticipates user needs, adapts to changing circumstances, and executes tasks proactively. For example, while a traditional AI assistant might need step-by-step instructions to book a flight, an AI Operator can independently search for options, consider your preferences, and complete the booking seamlessly.

Adaptability is another area where current AI systems fall short. Traditional AI is often rigid, requiring significant retraining or reprogramming to accommodate new tasks or environments. In contrast, the AI Operator learns continuously. Through advanced machine learning algorithms, it adapts to user behavior, refines its processes, and even learns new tasks over time. This adaptability makes it not just a tool but a dynamic partner capable of evolving alongside its user.

By resolving these challenges, the AI Operator paves the way for a more intuitive, efficient, and effective integration of AI into our lives. It breaks the boundaries of traditional systems, offering a solution that is as flexible and capable as the human imagination.

Enhancing Human-AI Collaboration

At the heart of the AI Operator's objectives is its ability to foster a new level of collaboration between humans and machines. While traditional AI systems often feel like tools, the AI Operator aims to function more like a colleague or partner. This shift is significant because it changes how we perceive and interact with technology.

Human-AI collaboration has always been limited by the fact that traditional AI systems rely heavily on explicit instructions. These systems operate in silos, performing tasks independently but lacking the ability to work alongside humans in a meaningful way. The AI Operator bridges this gap by combining intelligence with empathy, creating an environment where humans and AI can truly collaborate.

For example, in a business setting, an AI Operator could work alongside a marketing team. Instead of merely generating data or recommendations, it could actively participate in strategy meetings, offering insights, automating repetitive tasks, and even drafting proposals. This level of collaboration frees up the team to focus on creative and strategic aspects, making the entire process more efficient and impactful.

The AI Operator also excels in its ability to communicate effectively. Powered by advanced natural language processing, it understands context, tone, and intent. This allows it to engage in meaningful conversations, ask clarifying questions, and provide nuanced responses. Whether it's assisting a teacher in planning lessons or supporting a project manager in coordinating a team, the AI Operator's communication skills enhance its collaborative potential.

Moreover, the Operator's adaptability ensures that it can work seamlessly across various industries and roles. From healthcare and education to finance and logistics, it can tailor its functionality to meet the unique needs of each user. This versatility makes it an invaluable partner, capable of enhancing human capabilities in ways that traditional AI systems cannot.

In essence, the AI Operator transforms human-AI interaction from a one-sided relationship into a true partnership. By enhancing collaboration, it not only makes our lives easier but also unlocks new possibilities for innovation and growth.

Streamlining Complex Workflows

One of the most transformative aspects of the AI Operator is its ability to streamline complex workflows. In today's fast-paced world, managing multiple tasks and systems can be overwhelming. Whether it's coordinating a project, handling customer inquiries, or managing supply chains, the complexity of modern workflows often leads to inefficiencies and errors. The AI Operator is designed to tackle these challenges head-on, bringing order and efficiency to even the most intricate processes.

Traditional AI systems are often limited to handling specific tasks within a workflow. For instance, a customer service chatbot might handle initial inquiries but cannot resolve more complex issues that require input from multiple departments. Similarly, an AI-powered scheduling tool might help you book meetings but can't coordinate across multiple team members and time zones. These limitations create bottlenecks, forcing humans to step in and manually connect the dots.

The AI Operator eliminates these bottlenecks by taking a holistic approach to workflow management. It doesn't just execute individual tasks; it understands the bigger picture. For example, in a supply chain scenario, the AI Operator could manage inventory levels, coordinate with suppliers, track shipments, and even forecast demand. By automating these interconnected processes, it ensures that the workflow runs smoothly from start to finish.

Another key feature of the AI Operator is its ability to integrate with multiple platforms and systems. Through its advanced integration capabilities, it can connect disparate tools and data sources, creating a unified workflow. For instance, in a marketing campaign, the Operator could pull data from analytics platforms, automate email sequences, monitor social media engagement, and generate performance reports—all without requiring manual intervention.

The AI Operator's proactive functionality further enhances its ability to streamline workflows. Instead of waiting for users to identify issues or make decisions, it anticipates potential bottlenecks and takes preemptive action. For example, if a project deadline is approaching, the Operator might automatically allocate resources, send reminders, or adjust timelines to ensure that everything stays on track.

By streamlining complex workflows, the AI Operator not only saves time but also reduces stress and minimizes the risk of errors. It enables users to focus on high-value activities, knowing that the intricate details are being handled with precision and efficiency.

Fostering Accessibility Across Industries

One of the most exciting objectives of the AI Operator is its potential to democratize access to advanced AI capabilities. In the past, the benefits of AI were often limited to large organizations with the resources to develop and deploy complex systems. The AI Operator changes this dynamic by making cutting-edge technology accessible to businesses, professionals, and individuals across all industries.

Accessibility is a cornerstone of the AI Operator's design. It is built to be user-friendly, requiring minimal technical expertise to operate. This ease of use ensures that even small businesses and non-technical users can leverage its capabilities. For example, a small retail business could use the AI Operator to manage inventory, automate marketing campaigns, and provide personalized customer experiences—tasks that would otherwise require significant time and resources.

In education, the AI Operator can support teachers and students by automating administrative tasks, personalizing learning experiences, and providing real-time feedback. In healthcare, it can assist doctors and nurses by managing patient records, scheduling appointments, and even analyzing medical data. These applications demonstrate how the AI Operator can enhance productivity and effectiveness across diverse fields.

The Operator's adaptability also plays a crucial role in fostering accessibility. Its ability to learn and customize itself to meet the unique needs of different users ensures that it can be deployed in a wide range of contexts. Whether it's a farmer using the Operator to optimize crop yields or an entrepreneur using it to manage a startup, the possibilities are endless.

Furthermore, the AI Operator's affordability makes it a viable option for organizations of all sizes. By reducing the cost of entry, it enables more users to benefit from advanced AI capabilities. This democratization of technology has the potential to level the playing field, allowing smaller players to compete with larger organizations on equal footing.

In fostering accessibility, the AI Operator not only empowers individual users but also drives innovation and growth across industries. It opens up new opportunities, creates value, and ensures that the benefits of AI are shared widely.

Final Thoughts

The objectives of the AI Operator go beyond simply making technology more efficient. By resolving the challenges of traditional AI systems, enhancing human-AI collaboration, streamlining complex workflows, and fostering accessibility, it sets a new standard for what AI can achieve. It is not just a tool but a transformative force that has the potential to redefine how we live and work.

In this chapter, we've explored the key objectives that drive the AI Operator's design and functionality. These objectives are not just theoretical; they are practical solutions to real-world problems. As we move forward, the AI Operator will continue to evolve, unlocking new possibilities and pushing the boundaries of what's possible. It is a glimpse into the future of AI—a future that is collaborative, inclusive, and full of potential.

4. How the AI Operator Works

The Core Technology Behind AI Operators

To understand how the AI Operator works, it's important to delve into the core technologies that make it such a groundbreaking innovation. At its heart, the AI Operator combines advanced machine learning, natural language processing (NLP), computer vision, and reinforcement learning to perform tasks autonomously and intelligently. These technologies work together to enable the AI Operator to interact with digital interfaces, understand user intent, and execute tasks with remarkable precision.

One of the most significant advancements in AI technology is the ability to understand and process human language. Natural Language Processing (NLP) is a cornerstone of the AI Operator's functionality. It allows the system to comprehend commands, interpret context, and respond in a human-like manner. For example, if you ask the AI Operator to book a flight, it doesn't just take the command literally. It interprets your preferences, such as airline choice, seating preferences, and budget, to deliver a result that aligns with your needs.

In addition to NLP, machine learning plays a critical role in enabling the AI Operator to learn and adapt. Through continuous interaction with users, the system refines its understanding of tasks, user behavior, and contextual nuances. This learning capability allows the AI Operator to improve over time, becoming more efficient and accurate with every interaction.

Computer vision is another crucial component. This technology allows the AI Operator to "see" and interpret digital interfaces, such as websites and applications. By analyzing screenshots, the system can identify buttons, menus, forms, and other elements necessary for task execution. This visual processing capability ensures that the AI Operator can navigate and interact with interfaces just as a human would.

Lastly, reinforcement learning enables the AI Operator to make decisions based on outcomes. By evaluating the success or failure of its actions, the system learns to optimize its approach for future tasks. This ability to self-correct and improve makes the AI Operator a highly reliable and effective tool.

The "Computer-Using Agent" Model (CUA)

At the core of the AI Operator's functionality is a groundbreaking framework known as the "Computer-Using Agent" (CUA) model. This model represents a significant leap in AI capabilities, enabling the Operator to perform tasks that go beyond the limitations of traditional systems. The CUA model integrates natural language processing, vision-based interaction, and advanced decision-making algorithms to create a system that can mimic human interaction with digital interfaces.

The CUA model is unique because it allows the AI Operator to interact with Graphical User Interfaces (GUIs) in much the same way a human would. Unlike traditional AI systems that rely heavily on APIs for integration, the CUA model uses a virtual browser and simulated inputs to navigate websites, fill out forms, and complete transactions. This approach makes the AI Operator incredibly versatile, as it can function in environments where APIs are unavailable or limited.

One of the key innovations of the CUA model is its ability to interpret visual input. Using advanced computer vision algorithms, the

Operator can analyze screenshots of digital interfaces and identify actionable elements. For example, it can locate a "Buy Now" button on an e-commerce site, determine its position, and click on it to complete a purchase. This capability eliminates the need for specialized integrations, making the AI Operator a more flexible and adaptable solution.

Another important aspect of the CUA model is its integration with reinforcement learning. The Operator evaluates the outcomes of its actions and adjusts its strategies accordingly. For instance, if it encounters an error while filling out a form, it will analyze the issue, learn from the experience, and avoid making the same mistake in the future. This continuous improvement process ensures that the AI Operator becomes more efficient and effective over time.

The CUA model also incorporates a robust natural language understanding component. This allows the Operator to process complex commands, ask clarifying questions, and provide meaningful feedback. Whether it's scheduling a meeting, managing inventory, or drafting an email, the AI Operator's ability to understand and execute user intent is unparalleled.

Understanding Interface Interaction and Visual Input

One of the most impressive capabilities of the AI Operator is its ability to interact with digital interfaces in a human-like manner. This is achieved through a combination of interface interaction techniques and visual input processing.

The AI Operator uses a virtual browser to navigate websites and applications. It simulates mouse movements, clicks, and keyboard inputs to perform tasks just as a human would. For example, if you ask the Operator to book a table at a restaurant, it will open the restaurant's website, locate the reservation form, fill in the necessary details, and confirm the booking. This level of interaction is made possible by the system's ability to interpret and act on visual input.

Visual input processing is a critical component of the AI Operator's functionality. By analyzing screenshots of digital interfaces, the system can identify key elements such as buttons, text fields, and dropdown menus. Advanced computer vision algorithms enable the Operator to recognize these elements regardless of their layout or design. This ensures that the system can adapt to different interfaces and perform tasks consistently.

The AI Operator's ability to process visual input extends beyond simple recognition. It can also understand the context and purpose of interface elements. For instance, if it encounters a "Submit" button, it knows that clicking it will complete an action. Similarly, if it sees a "Captcha" verification, it will pause and alert the user for input. This contextual understanding ensures that the Operator can handle complex tasks with minimal user intervention.

Another noteworthy feature is the Operator's ability to handle dynamic interfaces. Many websites and applications use dynamic content that changes based on user interactions. The AI Operator's real-time processing capabilities allow it to adapt to these changes, ensuring seamless task execution. Whether it's navigating a multi-step form or responding to a pop-up notification, the Operator can handle it all.

Backend Processes: Decision-Making and Execution

The true strength of the AI Operator lies in its backend processes, which enable it to make decisions and execute tasks with precision. These processes combine data analysis, machine learning, and decision-making algorithms to deliver a seamless user experience.

When the AI Operator receives a command, the first step is to analyze the input. Using natural language processing, it identifies the user's intent and breaks down the task into actionable steps. For example, if the command is to book a flight, the Operator will identify the necessary parameters, such as departure city, destination, dates, and budget.

Once the task is defined, the Operator uses its decision-making algorithms to determine the best course of action. This involves evaluating multiple options, weighing pros and cons, and selecting the most optimal solution. For instance, when searching for flights, the Operator might compare prices across different airlines, consider layover times, and prioritize direct flights to find the best option.

The execution phase begins once a decision is made. The Operator uses its interface interaction capabilities to navigate digital platforms, enter information, and complete the task. Throughout this process, it continuously monitors for errors or unexpected issues. If an error occurs, the Operator analyzes the problem, adjusts its approach, and retries the action. This self-correcting mechanism ensures a high level of reliability.

The backend processes also include a feedback loop that enables the Operator to learn from its actions. By analyzing the outcomes of its tasks, the system identifies areas for improvement and updates its strategies accordingly. This continuous learning process ensures that the Operator becomes more efficient and effective over time.

Balancing Autonomy with User Oversight

While the AI Operator is designed to function autonomously, it also incorporates mechanisms to ensure user oversight and control. This balance between autonomy and oversight is critical for maintaining trust and ensuring the system's reliability.

One way the AI Operator achieves this balance is by providing real-time updates on its actions. Users can monitor the Operator's progress through a dashboard, which displays the tasks being performed, the steps completed, and any issues encountered. This transparency allows users to stay informed and intervene if necessary.

The Operator also includes a pause-and-confirm feature for sensitive tasks. For example, if a task involves entering payment information or making a significant purchase, the system will pause and request user confirmation before proceeding. This ensures that users retain control over critical decisions.

Additionally, the AI Operator is designed to handle exceptions gracefully. If it encounters a situation where it cannot proceed, it alerts the user and provides detailed information about the issue. This proactive communication ensures that tasks are completed accurately and efficiently.

Another important aspect of user oversight is customization. The AI Operator allows users to define preferences, set boundaries, and customize its behavior. For instance, users can specify spending limits for financial transactions or restrict access to certain types of content. This level of customization ensures that the Operator aligns with individual needs and values.

Final Thoughts

Understanding how the AI Operator works reveals the incredible complexity and ingenuity behind this technology. From its core technologies and the CUA model to its interface interaction and backend processes, every aspect of the AI Operator is designed to deliver autonomy, adaptability, and efficiency. By balancing advanced capabilities with user oversight, it offers a solution that is both powerful and trustworthy.

In this chapter, we've explored the inner workings of the AI Operator, shedding light on the technologies and processes that make it such a revolutionary tool. As we move forward, it becomes clear that the AI Operator is not just a technological marvel but a catalyst for transforming how we interact with the digital world. It's a glimpse into the future of AI—a future that is intelligent, collaborative, and deeply integrated into our lives.

5. Tasks the AI Operator Can Handle

Automating Repetitive and Mundane Tasks

In every aspect of life, whether personal or professional, repetitive tasks consume a significant portion of our time and energy. These tasks, though essential, often lack the need for human creativity or decision-making and can quickly lead to burnout. This is where the AI Operator comes in. By automating these repetitive and mundane tasks, it allows individuals and businesses to focus on more meaningful and high-value activities.

One of the most significant capabilities of the AI Operator is its ability to handle repetitive administrative work. Think about how much time you spend every day sorting through emails, organizing schedules, or inputting data into spreadsheets. The AI Operator can take over these tasks with remarkable efficiency. For example, it can filter your emails, prioritize the most important ones, and even draft responses based on your communication style. Similarly, it can manage your calendar by scheduling meetings, resolving conflicts, and sending out reminders.

In a business setting, automation by the AI Operator can streamline workflows and reduce operational costs. Tasks like generating reports, updating databases, and processing invoices can be completed in a fraction of the time it would take a human. Moreover, the AI Operator's ability to learn and adapt means that it becomes more efficient over time, identifying patterns and optimizing processes without requiring constant supervision.

This capability is particularly valuable in industries like customer service, where repetitive inquiries often dominate the workload. The AI Operator can handle common customer questions, such as order tracking or return policies, freeing up human agents to address more complex issues. By taking over these mundane tasks, the AI Operator not only saves time but also improves overall productivity and job satisfaction.

Web Navigation and Form Completion

Navigating websites and completing forms are tasks that might seem simple but can quickly become tedious, especially when done repeatedly. The AI Operator excels in this area, offering a level of efficiency and accuracy that far surpasses human capabilities.

At its core, the AI Operator is designed to mimic human interaction with digital interfaces. Using advanced computer vision and natural language processing, it can navigate websites, locate relevant information, and complete forms just as a human would. For instance, if you need to sign up for a webinar, the AI Operator can fill out the registration form, select your preferences, and submit the details without requiring your input at every step.

One of the standout features of the AI Operator is its ability to handle dynamic and complex web interfaces. Unlike traditional automation tools that rely on pre-programmed scripts, the AI Operator uses its visual input capabilities to adapt to changes in website design or layout. This means it can function effectively even on platforms where the structure is frequently updated.

In addition to navigating websites, the AI Operator can automate form completion across a wide range of applications. Whether it's applying for jobs, submitting expense reports, or filling out surveys, the Operator ensures that the process is quick, accurate, and hassle-free. This capability is particularly useful for businesses that need to process large volumes of forms regularly, such as loan applications or customer feedback forms.

The AI Operator's proficiency in web navigation and form completion not only saves time but also reduces the risk of errors. By automating these tasks, it ensures consistency and accuracy, enabling users to focus on more strategic or creative activities.

Personal and Business Productivity Tasks

The AI Operator is more than just a tool for automation; it is a productivity enhancer designed to simplify both personal and professional life. By taking on a wide range of productivity tasks, it helps users optimize their time and achieve their goals more effectively.

In a personal context, the AI Operator acts as a digital assistant, managing tasks like setting reminders, organizing to-do lists, and even planning events. For instance, if you're hosting a dinner party, the Operator can help you create a shopping list, send out invitations, and schedule reminders for preparation. Its ability to learn from your preferences means that it can anticipate your needs and provide proactive support.

For professionals, the AI Operator is a game-changer. It can assist with project management by tracking deadlines, assigning tasks, and monitoring progress. For example, a marketing manager could use the Operator to coordinate a campaign, ensuring that all team members are aligned and that tasks are completed on time. By automating these administrative tasks, the Operator allows professionals to focus on strategy and creativity.

Another area where the AI Operator excels is in managing communications. It can draft emails, schedule meetings, and even prepare presentation materials based on user inputs. Imagine having an assistant that not only reminds you of an important meeting but also prepares the agenda and sends follow-up emails to attendees—that's the level of productivity the AI Operator brings to the table.

The AI Operator's ability to enhance productivity is particularly valuable in today's fast-paced world, where multitasking has become the norm. By automating routine tasks and streamlining workflows, it empowers users to achieve more in less time.

E-Commerce Assistance and Online Transactions

As e-commerce continues to grow, managing online transactions has become a significant part of our daily lives. Whether it's ordering groceries, booking travel, or purchasing gifts, these tasks often require navigating multiple platforms and managing a variety of details. The AI Operator simplifies this process, offering a seamless and efficient solution for e-commerce activities.

One of the key strengths of the AI Operator is its ability to interact directly with e-commerce platforms. Using its web navigation capabilities, it can browse products, compare prices, and add items to your cart based on your preferences. For example, if you're planning a vacation, the Operator can search for flights, compare hotel options, and even book activities at your destination. It handles all the details, ensuring that you get the best deals without spending hours searching.

The AI Operator also excels in managing recurring purchases. By learning your buying habits, it can automate tasks like ordering groceries or renewing subscriptions. Imagine never having to worry about running out of household essentials because the Operator ensures they are delivered to your doorstep on time.

Security is a top priority when it comes to online transactions, and the AI Operator is designed with robust safeguards to protect user data. It uses encrypted channels to process payments and ensures that sensitive information, such as credit card details, is handled securely. Additionally, it includes a pause-and-confirm feature for high-value transactions, giving users the final say before completing a purchase.

Businesses can also benefit from the AI Operator's e-commerce capabilities. Retailers can use it to automate inventory management, process customer orders, and even analyze sales data for insights. By streamlining these operations, the Operator helps businesses save time and improve efficiency.

The AI Operator's e-commerce assistance is not just about convenience; it's about creating a seamless and enjoyable shopping experience. Whether you're a busy professional or a small business owner, the Operator ensures that online transactions are quick, secure, and stress-free.

Integrating with IoT for Seamless Automation

The Internet of Things (IoT) has revolutionized how we interact with our environment, connecting devices to create smart homes, offices, and cities. The AI Operator takes this concept to the next level by integrating with IoT devices to deliver seamless automation across various aspects of life.

In a smart home setting, the AI Operator can act as a central hub, managing everything from lighting and temperature to security and entertainment. For instance, it can adjust the thermostat based on your schedule, turn off lights when you leave the house, and even brew your morning coffee. By integrating with IoT devices, the Operator creates a connected ecosystem that enhances convenience and efficiency.

In the workplace, the AI Operator can integrate with IoT devices to optimize operations. For example, it can manage energy usage by controlling smart lighting and HVAC systems, ensuring that resources are used efficiently. It can also monitor IoT-enabled machinery in manufacturing settings, identifying maintenance needs and preventing downtime.

The AI Operator's ability to integrate with IoT extends beyond individual devices. It can connect entire systems, creating a unified network that operates seamlessly. For instance, in a smart city, the Operator could coordinate traffic signals, manage public transportation schedules, and monitor environmental conditions to improve urban living.

Security and privacy are critical considerations when integrating with IoT, and the AI Operator includes robust measures to address these concerns. It uses encrypted communication channels to protect data and allows users to customize access controls for different devices. This ensures that the benefits of IoT integration are delivered without compromising user safety.

By integrating with IoT, the AI Operator transforms the way we interact with our environment. It creates a world where devices work together harmoniously, delivering unparalleled convenience and efficiency.

Final Thoughts

The tasks the AI Operator can handle are as diverse as they are impactful. From automating repetitive work to navigating complex web interfaces, enhancing productivity, managing e-commerce transactions, and integrating with IoT, the Operator proves itself to be a versatile and indispensable tool. Its ability to learn, adapt, and execute tasks with precision ensures that it meets the needs of both individuals and businesses.

In this chapter, we've explored the wide-ranging capabilities of the AI Operator and how it simplifies and enhances daily life. As we look ahead, it's clear that the Operator is not just a tool for convenience but a transformative force that redefines what's possible in the digital age. With the AI Operator by your side, the possibilities are endless.

6. Advantages of the AI Operator

Time-Saving and Improved Efficiency

Time is one of our most valuable resources, yet it often feels like there isn't enough of it. Whether it's managing work responsibilities, handling personal tasks, or juggling both, the sheer number of repetitive and time-consuming activities we face can be overwhelming. The AI Operator is designed to address this exact problem by streamlining processes and optimizing workflows, ultimately saving users countless hours.

One of the AI Operator's standout features is its ability to automate routine tasks. For instance, instead of manually sorting through hundreds of emails, the Operator can categorize, prioritize, and even respond to messages based on user-defined criteria. In a professional setting, it can take over mundane tasks like generating reports, scheduling meetings, or updating spreadsheets, freeing up employees to focus on more strategic work.

Efficiency is another hallmark of the AI Operator. Unlike humans, who may experience fatigue or distractions, the Operator performs tasks with consistent speed and accuracy. It can complete activities in a fraction of the time it would take a person, from filling out online forms to navigating complex workflows. This efficiency is particularly beneficial in high-pressure environments where deadlines are tight, and precision is critical.

In industries like healthcare, logistics, and customer service, the time-saving benefits of the AI Operator are even more pronounced. For example, a healthcare provider might use the Operator to automate appointment scheduling, allowing staff to focus on patient care. In logistics, it can optimize supply chain management by tracking shipments, managing inventory, and predicting demand patterns. By handling these time-consuming activities, the AI Operator ensures that resources are used more effectively, driving both productivity and efficiency.

Boosting Productivity for Individuals and Businesses

Productivity is the cornerstone of success, both for individuals striving to meet their goals and businesses aiming to stay competitive. The AI Operator is a powerful tool for boosting productivity by taking on repetitive tasks, streamlining workflows, and enabling users to achieve more in less time.

For individuals, the Operator acts as a personal assistant that can manage day-to-day responsibilities. Whether it's organizing a calendar, setting reminders, or drafting emails, the Operator ensures that tasks are completed efficiently and on time. By automating these responsibilities, individuals can focus their energy on more meaningful activities, such as pursuing creative projects, learning new skills, or spending quality time with loved ones.

Businesses stand to gain even more from the productivity-enhancing capabilities of the AI Operator. By integrating it into their operations, companies can reduce bottlenecks, minimize errors, and improve overall efficiency. For instance, in a sales department, the Operator could automate lead generation, follow-up emails, and data entry, allowing sales professionals to focus on building relationships with clients. In manufacturing, it could monitor equipment performance, predict maintenance needs, and optimize production schedules to maximize output.

Another key advantage of the AI Operator is its ability to operate 24/7 without breaks. This is particularly valuable for global businesses that need to cater to customers across different time zones. With the Operator handling customer inquiries, processing orders, and managing backend operations around the clock, businesses can maintain continuity and deliver better service.

The productivity boost provided by the AI Operator is not just about getting more done; it's about doing the right things. By automating low-value tasks and enabling users to focus on high-value activities, the Operator helps individuals and businesses achieve their goals more effectively.

Creating More Free Time for High-Value Activities

In today's fast-paced world, finding time for high-value activities can be challenging. Whether it's strategizing for a business, nurturing personal relationships, or pursuing hobbies, these activities often take a backseat to daily responsibilities. The AI Operator addresses this issue by taking over mundane and repetitive tasks, giving users more time to focus on what truly matters.

For professionals, this means being able to dedicate more time to strategic thinking, innovation, and leadership. Instead of spending hours managing schedules or generating reports, they can focus on developing new ideas, solving complex problems, or mentoring their teams. This shift not only enhances individual productivity but also drives organizational success.

On a personal level, the AI Operator can significantly improve work-life balance. By automating household chores, managing online transactions, or organizing personal schedules, it frees up time for users to spend with their families, pursue hobbies, or simply relax. For instance, instead of spending an evening planning a vacation, users can let the Operator handle the logistics while they enjoy quality time with loved ones.

The ability to focus on high-value activities has a profound impact on overall well-being. Studies have shown that individuals who have more time for meaningful activities experience lower stress levels, greater job satisfaction, and improved mental health. By taking care of routine responsibilities, the AI Operator enables users to lead more fulfilling and balanced lives.

Enhancing Accuracy and Reducing Human Error

Human error is an unavoidable aspect of manual work, particularly when tasks are repetitive, time-sensitive, or require a high level of attention to detail. Errors can range from minor mistakes, such as typos in a document, to significant issues, such as miscalculations in financial data or incorrect order processing. The AI Operator addresses this challenge by performing tasks with unmatched accuracy and consistency.

One of the key advantages of the AI Operator is its ability to eliminate errors in data-intensive tasks. For example, in industries like finance and accounting, the Operator can manage tasks such as reconciling accounts, generating invoices, and preparing financial reports. By automating these processes, it ensures that calculations are accurate and compliant with regulations. This not only saves time but also reduces the risk of costly mistakes.

In customer service, the AI Operator's accuracy ensures that inquiries are handled promptly and correctly. Whether it's processing returns, updating account information, or resolving issues, the Operator's ability to follow predefined protocols minimizes errors and enhances the customer experience. Similarly, in healthcare, the Operator can assist with tasks like managing patient records, scheduling appointments, and analyzing medical data, ensuring that critical information is handled with precision.

The Operator's consistency is another key factor in reducing errors. Unlike humans, who may become fatigued or distracted, the Operator performs tasks with the same level of accuracy every time. This reliability is particularly valuable in high-stakes environments where mistakes can have significant consequences.

By enhancing accuracy and reducing human error, the AI Operator not only improves efficiency but also builds trust. Users can rely on the Operator to handle critical tasks with precision, giving them peace of mind and confidence in their work.

Democratizing Access to Advanced AI Capabilities

Traditionally, the benefits of advanced AI have been limited to large corporations and tech-savvy users with the resources to develop and deploy complex systems. The AI Operator changes this dynamic by making cutting-edge technology accessible to a broader audience, including small businesses, entrepreneurs, and individual users.

One of the ways the AI Operator democratizes access is through its user-friendly design. Unlike traditional AI systems that require extensive programming knowledge or technical expertise, the Operator is designed to be intuitive and easy to use. With its natural language interface, users can interact with the Operator as they would with a human assistant, making it accessible even to those with limited technical skills.

Affordability is another key factor in democratizing access. By offering the AI Operator at a competitive price point, developers ensure that businesses and individuals of all sizes can benefit from its capabilities. For example, a small business owner could use the Operator to automate tasks like managing inventory, processing orders, and responding to customer inquiries, enabling them to compete with larger companies without incurring significant costs.

The AI Operator's adaptability also plays a crucial role in expanding access. Its ability to learn and customize itself to meet the unique needs of different users ensures that it can be deployed in a wide range of contexts. Whether it's a teacher using the Operator to personalize lesson plans or a farmer optimizing crop yields, the possibilities are endless.

By democratizing access to advanced AI capabilities, the AI Operator levels the playing field and fosters innovation across industries. It empowers individuals and businesses to harness the power of AI, driving growth, efficiency, and success.

Final Thoughts

The advantages of the AI Operator are both transformative and far-reaching. From saving time and boosting productivity to enhancing accuracy and democratizing access, it offers solutions to some of the most pressing challenges faced by individuals and businesses today. By taking on repetitive tasks, enabling users to focus on high-value activities, and delivering consistent results, the Operator redefines what's possible in the digital age.

In this chapter, we've explored how the AI Operator enhances efficiency, improves productivity, and creates opportunities for innovation and growth. As we move forward, it's clear that the Operator is not just a tool for convenience but a catalyst for change, empowering users to achieve more and live better.

7. Challenges with the AI Operator

Privacy and Security Concerns

While the AI Operator holds immense potential to transform industries and daily life, it is not without its challenges. At the forefront of these challenges are privacy and security concerns, which are critical issues in a world increasingly reliant on digital systems. Users entrust AI Operators with sensitive data—from personal information and financial details to business-critical data. The stakes are high, and any mishandling of this information can lead to severe consequences, including identity theft, financial fraud, or corporate espionage.

One of the biggest concerns is data storage and access. The AI Operator requires access to large amounts of data to function effectively, often including personal preferences, browsing history, and task-related information. This raises the question: Where is this data stored, and how securely? Without robust encryption protocols and secure storage mechanisms, this data becomes vulnerable to breaches.

Another aspect is data transmission. AI Operators often communicate with multiple platforms and systems, transferring information across networks. These interactions need to be safeguarded against interception or unauthorized access. For example, when the AI Operator processes a payment or shares sensitive files, it must ensure that all communications occur over secure channels.

Moreover, the AI Operator's ability to learn from user interactions adds another layer of complexity. While this adaptability is a key strength, it also means that the Operator is constantly collecting and analyzing user data. Striking a balance between personalization and privacy is a delicate task. Developers must implement transparent data collection practices and give users control over what information is shared and stored.

Finally, there is the concern of third-party access. Many AI Operators integrate with external platforms to perform tasks, such as making purchases or booking appointments. These integrations can expose user data to third-party vendors, raising questions about how this information is handled and whether it is protected.

Handling Sensitive Information Safely

The ability of the AI Operator to manage sensitive information is one of its defining features—but it is also one of its greatest challenges. Handling sensitive data, such as financial credentials, medical records, or legal documents, requires a level of precision and security that leaves no room for error.

One challenge is ensuring the safe storage of sensitive data. For example, when users provide their credit card information or medical history, they need to trust that this data is encrypted and stored in a way that prevents unauthorized access. Developers must implement state-of-the-art security protocols to safeguard this information.

Another critical aspect is data transmission. The AI Operator must ensure that sensitive information is transmitted securely between systems. This involves using encrypted channels, such as HTTPS and Secure Sockets

Layer (SSL) protocols, to protect data from being intercepted during transmission. Without these measures, sensitive information could be compromised, leading to potentially catastrophic consequences.

User authentication is another key area of focus. The AI Operator must verify the identity of users before granting access to sensitive data or performing critical tasks. Multi-factor authentication (MFA) can add an additional layer of security, ensuring that only authorized users can interact with the system.

Transparency and user control are also vital. Users should be informed about how their sensitive data is being used and given the ability to manage it. For instance, they should be able to delete their data or restrict access to certain types of information. This not only enhances security but also builds trust between the user and the AI Operator.

Despite these safeguards, challenges remain. For example, if the Operator makes an error while handling sensitive data, such as entering incorrect payment information or sharing confidential files with the wrong recipient, the consequences can be significant. Addressing these risks requires rigorous testing, continuous monitoring, and robust error-handling mechanisms.

Limitations in Complex Interfaces and Tasks

The AI Operator's ability to navigate interfaces and execute tasks is one of its greatest strengths—but it's not without limitations. While the Operator excels in handling straightforward workflows, it can struggle with complex interfaces and multi-step tasks that require a high degree of contextual understanding.

One limitation lies in dynamic and highly customized interfaces. Websites and applications often change their layouts, add new elements, or introduce interactive features. While the AI Operator uses computer vision and machine learning to adapt to these changes, there are scenarios where it may misinterpret visual elements or fail to locate critical components. For instance, if a website introduces a CAPTCHA or a multi-layered dropdown menu, the Operator might require user intervention to proceed.

Another challenge is task prioritization in multi-step workflows. While the Operator can follow predefined instructions, complex tasks that involve multiple dependencies or require judgment can pose difficulties. For example, coordinating a multi-city business trip might involve balancing flight schedules, hotel availability, and meeting times. While the Operator can handle individual components, integrating them into a cohesive plan may require human oversight.

Moreover, the Operator's reliance on digital interfaces can be a limitation in itself. Tasks that involve integrating with non-digital systems, such as manual processes or physical documents, remain outside its scope. For example, while the Operator can manage digital invoices, it cannot process a physical receipt without additional tools like document scanners or optical character recognition (OCR) software.

These limitations highlight the importance of continuous improvement and user collaboration. Developers must invest in training the Operator to handle increasingly complex scenarios, while users must be prepared to provide guidance or step in when necessary. By working together, humans and AI Operators can overcome these challenges and achieve more robust outcomes.

Ethical Concerns in Autonomous Decision-Making

One of the most debated aspects of AI technology is its ethical implications, particularly when it comes to autonomous decision-making. The AI Operator's ability to act independently raises questions about accountability, fairness, and the potential for unintended consequences.

A primary concern is the issue of bias. AI systems, including the AI Operator, learn from data. If this data contains biases—whether related to gender, race, socioeconomic status, or other factors—the Operator may inadvertently perpetuate these biases in its decision-making. For instance, if the Operator is used in a hiring process and the training data includes biased hiring practices, it could result in unfair or discriminatory outcomes.

Another ethical concern is the transparency of decision-making processes. When the AI Operator makes an autonomous decision, such as approving a loan application or prioritizing tasks, it's important for users to understand how and why the decision was made. This requires developers to build systems that provide clear explanations for their actions, a concept known as explainable AI (XAI).

The potential for misuse is another challenge. In the wrong hands, the AI Operator could be used to automate malicious activities, such as phishing attacks, unauthorized surveillance, or the dissemination of misinformation. Developers and policymakers must work together to establish safeguards that prevent misuse and promote ethical deployment.

The issue of accountability also looms large. If the AI Operator makes a mistake or causes harm, who is responsible? Is it the user who deployed the system, the developer who created it, or the organization that owns it? Resolving these questions requires clear legal frameworks and guidelines to ensure accountability and protect all parties involved.

Finally, there is the concern of over-reliance on automation. While the AI Operator is designed to enhance productivity and efficiency, excessive reliance on it could lead to a loss of critical skills or a diminished capacity for independent decision-making. Striking a balance between automation and human oversight is essential to ensure that the Operator remains a tool for empowerment rather than a crutch.

Final Thoughts

The challenges associated with the AI Operator are significant but not insurmountable. Privacy and security concerns, the safe handling of sensitive information, limitations in complex tasks, and ethical considerations are all critical areas that require attention. By addressing these challenges head-on, developers, users, and policymakers can ensure that the AI Operator fulfills its potential while minimizing risks.

In this chapter, we've explored the hurdles that come with deploying and using the AI Operator. These challenges highlight the importance of continuous innovation, rigorous testing, and ethical accountability. As the technology evolves, it's crucial to approach it with both optimism and caution, recognizing its transformative potential while remaining mindful of its limitations. With the right safeguards in place, the AI Operator can become a trusted partner in shaping a better, more efficient future.

8. Impact on Jobs

Job Displacement and Automation Challenges

As AI technology continues to advance, the impact on jobs has become a topic of intense debate. The AI Operator, with its ability to automate complex workflows and perform tasks traditionally handled by humans, is no exception. While the technology holds immense promise, it also raises concerns about job displacement and the challenges that come with automation.

One of the most immediate effects of the AI Operator is the potential reduction in demand for certain roles. Jobs that involve repetitive, rule-based tasks are particularly vulnerable. For instance, data entry clerks, administrative assistants, and customer service representatives may find their roles increasingly automated. In industries such as manufacturing, logistics, and retail, the AI Operator's efficiency and accuracy can replace tasks traditionally performed by human workers, such as inventory management or order processing.

81

The ripple effects of automation extend beyond individual roles. Entire sectors may undergo transformation as businesses adopt AI Operators to streamline operations. For example, the transportation industry could see significant changes as autonomous systems take over fleet management and route optimization, potentially reducing the need for human dispatchers.

However, job displacement is not solely about losing positions; it's also about the psychological and societal impacts. Workers in roles affected by automation may experience anxiety, uncertainty, and a sense of obsolescence. Communities heavily reliant on certain industries could face economic challenges, requiring governments and organizations to step in with support measures.

Despite these challenges, it is essential to recognize that automation is not a zero-sum game. While the AI Operator may displace some roles, it also creates opportunities for new kinds of work—a concept we will explore further in this chapter.

New Opportunities in AI Management and Development

For every job that automation changes or replaces, it creates opportunities for new roles that were previously unimaginable. The AI Operator is no exception. Its widespread adoption has opened up a wealth of opportunities in AI management, development, and related fields.

One of the most obvious areas of growth is the development and maintenance of AI systems. As businesses and individuals rely more on AI Operators, there will be an increased demand for professionals who can design, train, and optimize these systems. Roles such as AI engineers, data scientists, and machine learning specialists will become even more critical in building and improving AI Operators to meet evolving needs.

In addition to technical roles, the rise of the AI Operator has created opportunities in AI management and strategy. Businesses adopting this technology require professionals who can oversee its implementation, integration, and ethical use. For example, an AI Operations Manager might be responsible for ensuring that the AI Operator aligns with organizational goals, complies with regulatory standards, and delivers value to stakeholders.

Another emerging field is AI ethics and governance. As the use of AI Operators becomes more prevalent, the need for professionals who can navigate the ethical and legal complexities of AI deployment grows. Roles in this area may involve developing guidelines for AI use, monitoring systems for bias, and ensuring that AI operates transparently and fairly.

Moreover, the AI Operator creates opportunities for entrepreneurs and innovators. With its ability to automate processes and reduce operational costs, small businesses and startups can leverage the technology to enter markets and compete on a level playing field with larger organizations. This democratization of technology fosters innovation and encourages the creation of new business models.

The shift toward AI-driven industries highlights the importance of adapting to change. While some roles may fade, the opportunities created by the AI Operator demonstrate that the future of work is not about replacement but transformation.

Reskilling and Upskilling for the AI Era

As the AI Operator reshapes the job landscape, reskilling and upskilling become critical to ensuring that workers remain relevant and competitive. Rather than viewing automation as a threat, individuals and organizations must embrace it as an opportunity to evolve and grow.

Reskilling refers to learning new skills to transition into different roles. For workers whose jobs are at risk of automation, reskilling programs can provide a pathway to new opportunities. For instance, a factory worker whose role has been replaced by an AI Operator might train in programming or AI system maintenance, enabling them to take on a new position in the same industry.

Upskilling, on the other hand, involves enhancing existing skills to adapt to changes within a current role. For example, a project manager might learn how to collaborate with AI

Operators to streamline workflows and improve efficiency. By acquiring these new competencies, individuals can enhance their value in the workplace and remain competitive in an AI-driven world.

Governments, educational institutions, and businesses all play a role in supporting reskilling and upskilling efforts. Governments can invest in workforce development programs and provide incentives for businesses to offer training opportunities. Educational institutions can update curricula to include AI-related subjects, ensuring that students are prepared for the future job market. Businesses, in turn, can offer in-house training programs, workshops, and certifications to help employees adapt to new technologies.

For individuals, lifelong learning is key. The rapid pace of technological change means that skills acquired today may become obsolete tomorrow. Staying curious, proactive, and adaptable is essential for navigating the evolving job landscape. Online platforms such as Coursera, Udemy, and LinkedIn Learning offer accessible resources for individuals to learn about AI, data analytics, and other emerging fields.

Reskilling and upskilling are not just about maintaining employability; they are about empowering individuals to thrive in a world where AI is an integral part of daily life. By embracing these opportunities, workers can turn challenges into stepping stones for success.

Striking a Balance Between Human and AI Roles

The rise of the AI Operator brings with it an important question: How do we strike the right balance between human and AI roles? While the Operator is designed to enhance productivity and efficiency, it is not meant to replace human creativity, empathy, and judgment. Finding this balance is crucial to ensuring that AI serves as a complement to human capabilities rather than a competitor.

One of the key strengths of humans is our ability to think creatively, solve complex problems, and build relationships. These qualities are difficult, if not impossible, for AI to replicate. The AI Operator excels in handling repetitive tasks, analyzing data, and providing insights, but it relies on humans to set goals, make strategic decisions, and drive innovation.

Collaboration is the cornerstone of striking this balance. In a workplace setting, the AI Operator can take over routine tasks, allowing employees to focus on higher-value activities. For example, an AI Operator might handle data analysis, freeing up analysts to interpret the results and develop actionable strategies. Similarly, in customer service, the Operator can manage initial inquiries, leaving human agents to resolve more complex or emotionally sensitive issues.

Transparency is another important factor. Users need to understand the capabilities and limitations of the AI Operator to use it effectively. For instance, while the Operator can provide recommendations based on data, it is ultimately up to humans to evaluate these suggestions and make informed decisions. Clear communication between humans and AI ensures that both parties can work together seamlessly.

Ethical considerations also play a role in balancing human and AI roles. Businesses and organizations must establish guidelines for how AI Operators are used, ensuring that they complement human efforts rather than replace them indiscriminately. This includes considering the broader impact on society, such as addressing job displacement and promoting inclusive practices.

Ultimately, the goal is not to create a world where humans are replaced by machines but to build one where humans and AI work together harmoniously. By leveraging the strengths of both, we can create a future that is more productive, innovative, and equitable.

Final Thoughts

The impact of the AI Operator on jobs is both profound and multifaceted. While it poses challenges in terms of job displacement and automation, it also creates new opportunities, necessitates reskilling, and highlights the importance of collaboration between humans and AI. By embracing change, investing in education and training, and fostering a culture of collaboration, we can navigate the transition to an AI-driven world successfully.

In this chapter, we've explored how the AI Operator is reshaping the job landscape, from the challenges of automation to the opportunities it creates. As we look ahead, it is clear that the future of work is not about humans versus machines but about humans and machines working together to achieve greater heights.

9. Impact on Businesses

Accelerating Business Growth with AI Automation

In today's competitive business landscape, growth is not just about expanding operations or increasing market share—it's about doing so efficiently and intelligently. The AI Operator plays a pivotal role in accelerating business growth by introducing automation that enhances productivity, reduces operational bottlenecks, and opens up new opportunities.

One of the most significant ways the AI Operator drives growth is through process automation. Businesses often deal with repetitive tasks that consume valuable time and resources. The AI Operator automates these tasks with speed and precision, freeing up employees to focus on strategic initiatives. For instance, in industries like manufacturing, the Operator can manage inventory levels, schedule production, and optimize supply chains, ensuring seamless operations and faster time-to-market for products.

Moreover, the AI Operator enables businesses to scale operations without a proportional increase in costs. By automating tasks such as data entry, reporting, and customer support, companies can handle higher volumes of work without the need for additional staff. This scalability is particularly beneficial for startups and small businesses that aim to grow quickly while keeping overheads low.

Another avenue for growth is innovation. With the AI Operator managing routine tasks, businesses can allocate more resources to research and development (R&D). For example, a pharmaceutical company could use the Operator to automate clinical trial data analysis, allowing researchers to focus on developing new treatments. This shift from reactive to proactive resource allocation is a game-changer for businesses aiming to innovate and lead in their industries.

Lastly, the AI Operator provides businesses with actionable insights through data analysis. By processing large datasets and identifying trends, it helps companies make informed decisions that drive growth. Whether it's identifying new market opportunities, optimizing marketing strategies, or forecasting demand, the AI Operator empowers businesses to act decisively and strategically.

Cost Reduction Through Efficiency Gains

One of the most immediate and tangible benefits of the AI Operator for businesses is cost reduction. By improving efficiency across various functions, the Operator helps companies save money while maintaining or even enhancing performance.

Labor costs are a significant expense for most businesses. The AI Operator reduces the need for manual labor in repetitive and time-consuming tasks. For instance, in the finance department, it can automate processes like invoice generation, expense tracking, and financial reporting. This not only reduces the workload for human employees but also minimizes errors that can lead to financial losses.

Operational efficiency is another area where the AI Operator delivers substantial cost savings. In logistics, for example, it can optimize delivery routes, track shipments in real-time, and predict maintenance needs for vehicles. These efficiencies lower fuel consumption, reduce delays, and prevent costly equipment breakdowns. Similarly, in retail, the Operator can manage inventory levels to avoid overstocking or stockouts, ensuring optimal use of resources.

Energy savings are an often-overlooked benefit of the AI Operator. By integrating with IoT devices, it can monitor and optimize energy usage in office buildings, warehouses, and factories. For example, the Operator might adjust lighting and HVAC systems based on occupancy levels, reducing energy waste and lowering utility bills.

In addition to these direct savings, the AI Operator minimizes the cost of human errors. Mistakes in data entry, order processing, or customer interactions can be costly for businesses. The Operator's precision and consistency ensure that these errors are significantly reduced, leading to better outcomes and fewer financial repercussions.

Over time, the cumulative savings from these efficiencies contribute to a healthier bottom line, enabling businesses to reinvest in growth, innovation, and employee development.

Revolutionizing Customer Service and Support

Customer service is a cornerstone of any successful business. In an era where customer expectations are higher than ever, the AI Operator is revolutionizing how companies deliver support and enhance the overall customer experience.

One of the key strengths of the AI Operator is its ability to provide 24/7 customer support. Unlike human agents who work in shifts, the Operator is always available to handle inquiries, resolve issues, and provide information. This round-the-clock availability is particularly valuable for global businesses that serve customers across different time zones.

The AI Operator's natural language processing capabilities enable it to engage with customers in a conversational and intuitive manner. Whether it's answering frequently asked questions, assisting with product recommendations, or troubleshooting technical issues, the Operator delivers responses that are contextually relevant and tailored to the customer's needs.

Personalization is another area where the AI Operator excels. By analyzing customer data, it can provide customized experiences that enhance satisfaction and loyalty. For example, an e-commerce company could use the Operator to recommend products based on a customer's browsing history, previous purchases, and preferences. This level of personalization creates a more engaging shopping experience and drives repeat business.

In addition to handling direct interactions, the AI Operator supports human agents by automating back-end tasks. For instance, it can summarize customer interactions, update CRM systems, and generate support tickets, allowing agents to focus on complex or high-value cases. This collaboration between humans and AI improves the efficiency and quality of customer service.

Finally, the AI Operator provides businesses with valuable insights into customer behavior and preferences. By analyzing interaction data, it identifies trends, pain points, and opportunities for improvement. These insights help companies refine their products, services, and support strategies, ensuring that they stay ahead of customer expectations.

Risks and Responsibilities in AI Deployment

While the AI Operator offers significant benefits for businesses, its deployment is not without risks and responsibilities. Companies must navigate these challenges carefully to maximize the advantages while minimizing potential downsides.

One of the primary risks is over-reliance on automation. While the AI Operator can handle many tasks efficiently, businesses must ensure that critical decisions and creative processes remain under human control. Over-automating operations can lead to a loss of human oversight, potentially resulting in errors, ethical lapses, or missed opportunities for innovation.

Another concern is data security and privacy. The AI Operator requires access to sensitive information to function effectively, from customer data to internal business records. Companies must implement robust security measures to protect this data from breaches and unauthorized access. Additionally, they must comply with regulations such as GDPR or CCPA, ensuring that data is handled transparently and responsibly.

Bias and fairness are also critical issues in AI deployment. The AI Operator learns from data, and if that data contains biases, the Operator may inadvertently perpetuate them. For instance, in hiring processes or customer service interactions, biased algorithms could lead to unfair outcomes. Businesses must invest in auditing and refining AI models to ensure that they operate fairly and inclusively.

Accountability is another challenge. When the AI Operator makes a mistake or causes harm, determining responsibility can be complex. Companies must establish clear guidelines for accountability, ensuring that employees, developers, and stakeholders understand their roles and responsibilities in AI deployment.

Finally, there is the risk of workforce disruption. As businesses adopt the AI Operator to automate tasks, they must consider the impact on employees whose roles are affected. Transparent communication, reskilling programs, and a commitment to supporting workers through the transition are essential to maintaining morale and fostering a positive workplace culture.

Despite these risks, the responsibilities associated with deploying the AI Operator also present opportunities for businesses to lead by example. By prioritizing ethical practices, transparency, and inclusivity, companies can build trust with customers, employees, and stakeholders while reaping the benefits of AI automation.

Final Thoughts

The AI Operator is transforming the way businesses operate, offering unparalleled advantages in growth, efficiency, customer service, and cost savings. However, its deployment also comes with risks and responsibilities that require careful consideration and proactive management.

In this chapter, we've explored how the AI Operator accelerates business growth, reduces costs, and revolutionizes customer service while highlighting the challenges that come with its adoption. As businesses navigate this transformative era, the key to success lies in leveraging the AI Operator's capabilities responsibly and strategically, ensuring that it serves as a catalyst for innovation and progress.

10. The Future of AI Operators

Emerging Trends and Technological Innovations

The journey of AI Operators has only just begun. As technology evolves at an unprecedented pace, the future of AI Operators promises to be more sophisticated, versatile, and impactful. Emerging trends and technological innovations are shaping the trajectory of these systems, ensuring that they become even more integral to our personal and professional lives.

One of the most exciting trends in AI is the integration of generative AI with AI Operators. By combining the creative capabilities of generative AI with the operational intelligence of AI Operators, future systems will be able to craft unique content, design solutions, and even simulate scenarios for strategic planning. For instance, an AI Operator could draft a complete marketing campaign, including visuals and messaging, based on a company's objectives and audience preferences.

Another key innovation is the development of multimodal AI. Currently, AI Operators rely primarily on text-based and visual inputs. However, future systems will incorporate multimodal capabilities, allowing them to process and respond to inputs in various forms, including voice, video, and even biometric data. Imagine an AI Operator that can analyze a video feed to monitor workplace safety or use voice commands to control IoT devices in real-time.

The evolution of edge computing will also play a significant role in advancing AI Operators. By processing data locally on devices rather than relying on cloud servers, edge computing enhances speed, reduces latency, and ensures greater privacy. This advancement is particularly important for industries like healthcare and finance, where real-time decision-making and data security are critical.

Another trend shaping the future of AI Operators is their increasing interoperability. Future systems will be designed to seamlessly integrate with diverse platforms, applications, and devices, creating a unified ecosystem. This interoperability will enable AI Operators to function as central hubs for managing various technologies, from smart home systems to enterprise software.

Finally, advances in reinforcement learning and neural networks will make AI Operators more autonomous and adaptive. These systems will not only execute tasks but also learn and improve from their experiences, becoming more efficient and effective over time. This continuous learning capability ensures that AI Operators remain relevant and valuable in an ever-changing world.

Expanding Use Cases Across Industries

The versatility of AI Operators means that their applications are virtually limitless. As technology advances, these systems will continue to find new use cases across industries, transforming how businesses and individuals operate.

In healthcare, AI Operators will revolutionize patient care and medical research. They will assist doctors by analyzing patient data, identifying potential diagnoses, and suggesting treatment plans. In addition, they will streamline administrative tasks such as appointment scheduling, billing, and record management. On the research front, AI

Operators will analyze vast datasets to accelerate drug discovery and identify trends in public health.

In education, AI Operators will create personalized learning experiences for students. By analyzing performance data, they will tailor lessons to individual needs, ensuring that every student receives the support they require. They will also assist educators by automating administrative tasks, such as grading assignments and managing schedules, allowing teachers to focus on instruction and mentorship.

The retail industry will also benefit from AI Operators. These systems will enhance the customer experience by providing personalized product recommendations, managing inventory, and optimizing supply chains. For example, an AI Operator could predict consumer demand for specific products and adjust stock levels accordingly, reducing waste and improving profitability.

In manufacturing, AI Operators will drive efficiency and innovation. They will monitor machinery for maintenance needs, optimize production schedules, and ensure quality control. By automating these processes, manufacturers can reduce downtime, increase output, and maintain high standards of quality.

The financial sector will leverage AI Operators for tasks such as fraud detection, investment analysis, and customer service. These systems will analyze transactions in real-time to identify suspicious activities, provide clients with personalized financial advice, and streamline processes like loan approvals and account management.

Even creative industries will find applications for AI Operators. Artists, writers, and designers will use these systems to generate ideas, refine their work, and manage their projects. For instance, an AI Operator could assist a novelist by suggesting plot developments, editing drafts, and organizing research materials.

The expansion of AI Operator use cases across industries highlights their transformative potential. By automating tasks, enhancing decision-making, and fostering innovation, these systems are poised to reshape the way we work and live.

Ensuring Ethical Development and Governance

As AI Operators become more powerful and pervasive, the need for ethical development and governance becomes increasingly urgent. These systems hold immense potential for positive change, but without proper oversight, they also pose risks that could undermine trust and societal well-being.

One of the most pressing ethical concerns is data privacy. AI Operators rely on vast amounts of data to function effectively, raising questions about how this data is collected, stored, and used. Developers must prioritize transparency and implement robust data protection measures to ensure that user information is handled responsibly. Users should have control over their data, with clear options to opt out of data collection or delete their information.

Bias in AI systems is another critical issue. AI Operators learn from datasets that may contain biases, leading to unfair or discriminatory outcomes. For example, an AI Operator used in hiring might inadvertently favor certain demographics based on biased training data. To address this, developers must rigorously test AI

Operators for bias and implement measures to ensure fairness and inclusivity.

Accountability is also a key consideration. When an AI Operator makes a mistake or causes harm, it must be clear who is responsible. Companies must establish accountability frameworks that define roles and responsibilities, ensuring that developers, users, and organizations share the burden of oversight.

Ethical governance extends beyond individual organizations. Policymakers and regulators must establish standards and guidelines for AI Operator deployment. These regulations should address issues such as data protection, transparency, and the ethical use of AI in decision-making processes. International cooperation will be crucial to creating a cohesive framework that promotes responsible AI development on a global scale.

Education and awareness are equally important. As AI Operators become more integrated into society, individuals must understand their capabilities, limitations, and implications. Public awareness campaigns, training programs, and educational initiatives can help bridge the knowledge gap and empower people to use AI Operators responsibly.

By ensuring ethical development and governance, we can maximize the benefits of AI Operators while minimizing their risks. This approach fosters trust, promotes fairness, and ensures that AI serves as a force for good.

Preparing Society for a World with AI Operators

The widespread adoption of AI Operators will have profound implications for society. To harness their potential while mitigating challenges, we must prepare individuals, organizations, and communities for a world where these systems are ubiquitous.

One of the first steps is to address workforce transitions. As AI Operators automate tasks, some jobs may become obsolete while others will evolve. Governments, businesses, and educational institutions must collaborate to provide reskilling and upskilling programs that equip workers with the skills needed for AI-driven industries. These initiatives should focus on technical skills, such as programming and data analysis, as well as soft skills like creativity and problem-solving.

Another critical area is education. Schools and universities must integrate AI literacy into their curricula, ensuring that students understand the fundamentals of AI technology, its applications, and its ethical implications. By fostering a generation of AI-literate individuals, we can build a society that is better equipped to leverage the benefits of AI Operators.

Public awareness campaigns can also play a vital role in preparing society. These initiatives should aim to demystify AI Operators, addressing common misconceptions and highlighting their potential benefits. By promoting informed discussions about AI, we can reduce fear and resistance to technological change.

Collaboration between stakeholders is essential for creating a supportive ecosystem for AI Operators. Governments must enact policies that encourage innovation while protecting public interests. Businesses should adopt best practices for AI deployment, prioritizing transparency, fairness, and inclusivity.

Researchers and developers must continue to push the boundaries of what AI Operators can achieve, guided by ethical principles.

Finally, individuals must take an active role in shaping the future of AI Operators. By staying informed, advocating for responsible AI use, and engaging with the technology, people can ensure that AI Operators align with their values and needs.

Final Thoughts

The future of AI Operators is bright, filled with opportunities to transform industries, improve lives, and drive innovation. Emerging trends and technological advancements will make these systems more powerful and versatile, while expanding use cases across industries will unlock new possibilities. However, the path forward requires careful consideration of ethical challenges and a collective effort to prepare society for a world with AI Operators.

In this chapter, we've explored the trajectory of AI Operators, from technological innovations to their societal impact. As we look ahead, it is clear that the future of AI Operators is not just about what they can do but about how we choose to use them. By embracing their potential responsibly and inclusively, we can create a future where AI Operators are not just tools but partners in building a better world.

Conclusion: Embracing the Era of AI Operators

The journey through the world of AI Operators has been one of discovery, exploration, and insight. From understanding what an AI Operator is to delving into its potential impacts on industries, jobs, and society, this book has aimed to provide a comprehensive view of this transformative technology.

We began by defining the AI Operator, positioning it as more than just a tool but a revolutionary system capable of automating tasks, learning from interactions, and collaborating with humans in meaningful ways. Its ability to act autonomously, adapt to new environments, and integrate seamlessly with various platforms marks a significant evolution from traditional AI systems.

In subsequent chapters, we explored the many facets of AI Operators:

1. The Need for AI Operators: Highlighting the challenges of traditional AI tools, we saw how the Operator addresses gaps such as limited autonomy, adaptability,

113

and scope, while paving the way for more intuitive and efficient interactions.

2. Objectives of the AI Operator: We examined how the Operator resolves current limitations, enhances collaboration, streamlines workflows, and fosters accessibility across industries.

3. How AI Operators Work: A deep dive into the technology behind the Operator revealed the intricate processes that enable it to mimic human interactions, process visual input, and execute complex tasks.

4. Tasks AI Operators Can Handle: From automating mundane tasks to integrating with IoT devices, the Operator's versatility was showcased, demonstrating its ability to transform both personal and professional environments.

5. Advantages of AI Operators: By saving time, improving productivity, and enhancing accuracy, these systems offer solutions to some of the most pressing challenges faced by individuals and businesses today.

6. Challenges with AI Operators: No technology is without its challenges. We addressed privacy concerns, ethical dilemmas, and limitations, underscoring the importance of responsible development and deployment.

7. Impact on Jobs and Businesses: While AI Operators may displace certain roles, they also create opportunities for innovation, reskilling, and industry transformation. For businesses, the Operator represents a catalyst for growth, efficiency, and customer satisfaction.

8. The Future of AI Operators: Emerging trends and expanding use cases show that the potential of AI Operators is far from being fully realized. However, their future must be guided by ethical principles, inclusivity, and collaboration.

Each of these chapters provided a building block for understanding the profound implications of AI Operators. Together, they form a narrative that underscores not just the technological possibilities but also the human considerations essential to embracing this new era.

The Role of AI Operators in Shaping Tomorrow

As we look ahead, it's clear that AI Operators will play a central role in shaping the future. Their impact will be felt across all facets of life, from how we work and communicate to how we innovate and solve global challenges.

In the workplace, AI Operators are set to become indispensable collaborators. They will not only automate repetitive tasks but also provide insights and recommendations that drive smarter decision-making. For industries such as healthcare, manufacturing, and education, these systems will unlock efficiencies, improve outcomes, and expand access to critical services. For example, an AI Operator in healthcare could help diagnose diseases faster, optimize treatment plans, and manage patient records seamlessly, saving lives and improving care delivery.

On a societal level, AI Operators have the potential to address some of humanity's most pressing challenges. From combating climate change through better resource management to enhancing disaster response efforts, these systems can analyze data at scale and execute actions with unparalleled speed. Their ability to process and interpret complex information makes them valuable allies in tackling issues that require both precision and agility.

For individuals, AI Operators represent an opportunity to lead more balanced and fulfilling lives. By taking over mundane responsibilities, these systems free up time for personal growth, creativity, and meaningful connections. They serve as enablers, empowering people to focus on what truly matters while maintaining control over their digital environments.

However, the role of AI Operators extends beyond practical applications. They are also catalysts for redefining how we think about human-machine collaboration. By fostering a partnership between humans and AI, these systems challenge traditional notions of what technology can and should do. They push us to envision a future where machines augment human potential rather than replace it, creating a symbiotic relationship that benefits all.

Final Thoughts on the Balance Between Innovation and Ethics

The rise of AI Operators brings with it an array of opportunities, but it also demands a commitment to responsible innovation. As we embrace this technology, we must navigate a delicate balance between harnessing its potential and addressing its ethical implications.

One of the most critical aspects of this balance is transparency. Users must understand how AI Operators function, what data they collect, and how decisions are made. This transparency builds trust and ensures that users remain informed and empowered. Developers and organizations have a responsibility to communicate clearly and openly about their AI systems, fostering accountability and user confidence.

Privacy and security are equally paramount. As AI Operators become more integrated into our lives, protecting sensitive data must be a top priority. Robust encryption, secure storage, and user-centric data controls are essential for safeguarding information and preventing misuse. At the same time, regulatory frameworks must evolve to address the unique challenges posed by AI, ensuring that its deployment aligns with societal values.

Bias and fairness are other critical considerations. AI Operators learn from data, and if that data is biased, the systems may perpetuate inequities. Developers must prioritize diversity and inclusivity in their training datasets, implementing measures to identify and mitigate bias. Ethical AI development is not just about avoiding harm; it's about actively promoting fairness and equality.

Finally, we must address the broader societal implications of AI Operators. As these systems transform industries and jobs, it is essential to support workers through reskilling programs and ensure that the benefits of AI are distributed equitably. Policymakers, businesses, and communities must collaborate to create an environment where technology uplifts rather than marginalizes.

The journey ahead is one of continuous learning and adaptation. As AI Operators evolve, so too must our understanding of their impact and our approach to their development. By prioritizing ethics, inclusivity, and collaboration, we can ensure that these systems contribute to a future that is not only technologically advanced but also deeply human.

Conclusion

The era of AI Operators is here, and it holds the promise of transforming our world in profound ways. These systems are more than just tools; they are partners in innovation, efficiency, and progress. By automating tasks, enhancing decision-making, and fostering collaboration, AI Operators have the potential to unlock new possibilities for individuals, businesses, and society as a whole.

However, with great power comes great responsibility. Embracing the era of AI Operators requires us to approach their development and deployment with care, foresight, and a commitment to ethical principles. It challenges us to think critically about how we use technology and what kind of future we want to create.

As we stand on the cusp of this new era, the path forward is clear: We must embrace AI Operators as enablers of progress while remaining vigilant stewards of their potential. By doing so, we can ensure that this transformative technology serves as a force for good, shaping a future that is as equitable and inspiring as it is innovative.

Copyright Information

AI Operator Simplified

Copyright © 2025 by Jaideep Parashar

www.jaideepparashar.com

DISCLAIMER

While all attempts have been made to verify the information provided in this publication, the author does not assume any responsibility for errors, omissions, or contrary interpretations of the subject.

The views expressed are those of the author alone, and should not be taken as expert instruction or commands. The reader is responsible for his or her own actions.

The author makes no representations or warranties with respect to the accuracy or completeness of the contents of this work and specifically disclaims all warranties, including without limitation warranties of fitness for a particular purpose. No warranty may be created or extended by sales or promotional materials. The advice and recipes contained herein may not be suitable for everyone and every situation. This work is sold with the understanding that the author is not engaged in rendering medical, legal or other professional advice or services. If professional assistance is required, the services of a competent professional person should be sought. The author shall not be liable for damages arising here from. That an individual, organization of website is referred to in this work as a citation and/or potential source of further information does not mean that the author endorses the information the individual, organization to website may provide or recommendations they/it may make. Further, readers should be aware that Internet websites listed in this work might have changed or disappeared between when this work was written and when it is read.

Adherence to all applicable laws and regulations, including international, federal, state, and local governing professional licensing, business practices, advertising, and all other aspects of doing business in any jurisdiction in the world is the sole responsibility of the purchaser or reader.

About the Author

Jaideep Parashar, a visionary researcher & keynote speaker in the field of artificial intelligence, holds a master's degree in Electronics and Communication Engineering, and certifications courses from IIT Delhi and London School of Business Administration. His professional journey is marked by unconventional decisions and approach. In 2019, Jaideep made the choice to leave his comfort zone of secure government job, setting out on a path to work for his passion in business and research.

Currently, he serves as the Founder and Director of ReThynk AI Innovation & Research Pvt Ltd, where his innovative thinking and strategic vision have driven significant contribution for the company. He is also recognized as the brain behind Vista Liberata, a venture known for its contributions to the Marketing Communications.

The LinkedIn Top Voice in Artificial Intelligence, IoT, Venture Capital and others, Jaideep is a prolific author with a portfolio of influential books including Master the Art of Successful Career, Startup Untold Story, When Startup Succeed, and the complete ChatGPT Prompt Series.

Beyond his professional endeavors, Jaideep is an avid marathon runner, yellow-belt holder in Taekwondo, prompt expert and an enthusiastic reader, having devoured over 1000 books. His passion for continuous learning and personal growth is evident in every aspect of his life, making him a true inspiration to aspiring professionals and entrepreneurs.

https://www.jaideepparashar.com/